SOUL Poetry

I0176790

Kiran Waqar

Hawa Adam

Lena Ginawi

Balkisa Abdikadir

Cool Islam Publications

www.coolislam.org

Table of Contents

Welcome

Kiran Waqar, Hawa Adam, Lena Ginawi, Balkisa Abdikadir

Welcome, Welcome, Welcome, Welcome, Welcome

Child your mother is calling you

Come mix into this melting pot

We invite the flavor, the culture, the warmth

Come to the land of the free

To the home of the brave

Whose land is this?

How far does your freedom go back?

Do you know the names of the tribes you stand on?

Who decides who stands here?

My torch is lit for you

I stand alone in the dark

Come join me

Come

My soil is ready for your footprints

This place is one for your feet to stomp all over the restrictions

Child come swim in this liquor of liberty

Let me tell you

I fought hard for my freedom

My children are dead

My mother is dead

My father is dead

My family is dead

I am alone

I cannot breathe

Tell me, who is truly welcome here?

Lady liberty teach us again

I'm still teaching with open arms,

Please join me, please hug me

Enrich me

Truly make me great again

Lady Liberty, you were built with broken chains at your feet

You were a gift that tried to erase the memory

Of a time when they brought darker folks than me

Iron clad with heads down, souls broken

Can your people welcome us without owning us?

Yes. I am a mother; you are my children.

I cannot own my own kin.

My family is deeper than countries and boundaries, my blood line is thicker than oceans.

Give me all those who ache to breathe in a space where they will not be beaten for daring to let their lungs expand.

Yes, I want your tired, poor, the ones yearning to breathe free.

Child breathe free

We can't breathe.

The walls they talk of building are closing in on us

Where is the freedom that you once gave out so graciously?

Why do you refuse us today when you accepted us yesterday?

You are welcome

I invite you who have suffered

To enjoy this freedom, to be fed

I'll let you in, have let them in

I held my torch for all to see when they drew close

That their travel had paid off

I am still prepared for the waves, the currents of people washing onto my beaches

Do you mean the pollution?

We are trash

We take up too much space

No one speaks up for us

We are the immigrants who stole your jobs

Who built your jobs

Oh, how you forget history

You turned away Jewish refugees and sent them back to Europe

Sent them back to the camps they had run from

But they were so close, waiting on the beaches of Florida

Full of hope, America would save them

You would save them

But we are a threat, **aren't we?**

That justifies it, **right?**

We are spies, a danger to national security

We were

We are

Scary

Dangerous

Foreign

But aren't we all your children?

It is time to make amends

Knock, knock, knock

We're still here

You're White

Hawa Adam and Balkisa Abdikadir

Hey Black girl, it's almost like you're.... white

What does that even mean?

That my voice is a little too high for my identity?

That I carry binders around instead of a bottle of Hennessey?

That my tongue articulates without an accent?

That I can't use slang?

Cause, girl, you got me bent!

Tell me, is white a remedy to the poison of blackness?

Is my coffee color too black and too strong?

Or do you call me white because I spend 4.99 on a vanilla bean Frappuccino?

Actually girl you should try the iced caramel macchiato

Does white to you mean educated, successful, satisfaction guaranteed?

Does it mean participating in extracurricular?

You know, doing the most, getting away with stuff

Being from a good family?

I have a good family

And I'm not white

I don't want this to be called white.

Certainly not the type of white that comes with white guilt.

The white of the past.

The white of colonialism, occupation, oppression.

The white of right now.

The white privileged

I'm not privileged

Don't call me white

Do you call me white because black means broken?

Let me tell you in this box of crayons black is the color most used, broken and left behind

But I am not a crayon that can be left behind

Let's rewind

It's our people who work the jobs you think you exceeded

So don't tell me we are no longer needed

Because I sign up for AP classes

Honors classes

I'm pursuing my high school education

College education

Even though no one in my family has a college level education

Hey black girl, it's almost like you're…

Black....

American Dream

Kiran Waqar and Hawa Adam

American Dream

♫ Star Spangled Banner ♫

America, the golden brick road to success. A place they had seen on TV screens, books and magazines.

Just the thought made their heart swell. They saw Americans whose eyes glittered with passion, whose souls were filled with hope of the future. They wanted that.

It was a place where their children's children could reach for the sky where they could reach for the sky.

A place where they were told to shoot for the moon so they would land among the stars. A place where the rags to riches story was as common as their veins which bled red, white and blue.

Where anything could happen regardless of race, sexuality or creed. America was their ticket to equality, opportunity, and liberty. It was the promise land!

♫ Star Spangled Banner Ends ♫

They wanted to be Americans

And they fought with every tooth and nail

Just to get here

Just to set foot on American soil

To walk the grounds that paved the way to clean water

Education

And a house

With a white picket fence

It was the stuff of legends.

Nothing could convince them that these legends were just myths

That the American dream was just a spark that would never become a flame

How could they have known that America would greet them with lower wages, angry stares and hateful words?

With an obstacle at every turn

Despite all of this, our parents still believed

So they passed on the dream like a family heirloom passed from

Generation

To generation

To generation

To us

Now they're fighting for the future of their children

So they push and push and push

For the next CEO

For the next president

For the star doctor

For the mother who could pay her rent

For them to find the secret key to the American dream

The one they were told they would get if they worked harder

Longer

And stronger

We are those children

The ones who have to become the next CEO

The next president

The star doctor

The mother who could pay her rent

We live our lives with the pressure of a thousand tons of bricks

Slowly crushing us with every breath

Every project

Club

Expectations

We have to succeed for ourselves and for them

While having societal and individual pressures closing in on us

We are becoming claustrophobic

We reach out for help with a confused shrug for an answer

They never went to the schools we go to now

Never experienced the emotions we feel now

Never lost their culture in the stereotypical girl

OMG

LOL

That's so fetch

They never had to navigate two worlds in one body

Drowning in so many identities without a single lifesaver

They never went through it

Facts

They never came home to the same old attacks

Quit it with the poetry! Don't you know that's no way to a doctor's degree?

Why are doing so much extra stuff?

Now you won't be able to focus on your grades enough

Why are you out so late?

Who's the boy? Was it your first date?

And you aren't that forgiving so I keep on giving and giving and giving to **your American Dream and our American nightmare**

But don't get us wrong

We love our parents

♫ America the Beautiful Begins ♫

Who fought with every tooth and nail to get us here

Who have given us opportunities we wouldn't have had

So don't think we're ungrateful to you

Or for that matter for our education

We value what we've been given

And hope to give it to the next generation

But where our past one has failed is not in the school system or in the parenting it's in

The American Dream

♫ …from sea to shining sea ♫

Wake Up America

Hawa Adam, Kiran Waqar, Lena Ginawi, Balkisa Abdikadir

September 11th, 2001

Wake up America, the enemy is here

The terrorist

The jihadists

Those A-rabs

The womanizers

The monsters

Those Bin laden's

The ones to watch out for

To surveil

To remove

To attack

But actually we're

The advocates

The award winners

The bilinguals

Hello

Hola

Bonjour

Guten tag

Assalamualaikum

We're the 4.0 Students

The honor roll students

The star athletes

But we're also the misunderstood

The ones to watch out for

To surveil

To remove

To attack

It was the first day of the 10th grade, my first day with the hijab in public. This hijab had the power to change me from Kiran Waqar, typical teen, to Kiran Waqar, an ambassador for all 1.6 billion Muslims.

March 21st, 2003

Fireworks were thrown into a Palestinian family's van

Flames burned brighter than the rockets' red glare

America, what are you celebrating?

April 6th, 2004

A woman's hijab is ripped off and she is verbally assaulted.

But she's dangerous, **riiight?** She deserves this, **riiiight?**

Wait, wait, wait, it's her body **right,** women should be able to do what they want, **right!**

So if you can show why can't we conceal?

August 6th, 2007

A chemical bomb is tossed at a mosque in Glendale Arizona

The bomb almost hit two Muslim Americans.

Imagine what could have happened,

Two mothers

Could have lost their sons

Two men

Could have lost their lives

But wait,

America, you don't care about our protection

because you're trying to protect yourselves from us

From me

I was walking home from school and you decided to cross on the other side of the street. Was the surface I walked on too hot for you to come near? Did you know that your look flamed the fire of insecurities within me?

August 24th, 2010

A taxi driver picks up Michael Enright, his first passenger of the day

It was an average ride until he uttered the word **'Muslim'**

Michael Enright, slashes the taxi drivers face, not once.

Not twice.

What a price to pay for the freedom of your rights?

What happened to our freedom of religion?

The ones promised to you, and you, and you?

And me?

What about me?

It's the first day of school, I am the only Muslim girl with the hijab. I can feel everyone's eyes, razor sharp, their lips forming questions. Who knew curiosity could cut so deep? I just wanted to curl up in a corner.

February 10th, 2010

Imagine you're a Muslim going to your house of prayer, seeing a cross and the words Muslims Go Home written with red paint on the white walls.

Go home they said? Go home where?

The hospital where I was born?

The city where I was raised?

We aren't just Muslims

We're American Muslims

Equal in every way

I heard the words roll off of his tongue "You Moslems are the reason the airport lines are so long. You bombers" He was drunk but a drunk mind speaks a sober heart

These are the things we see, hear, and experience daily

And now you've know of these:

Hidden crimes

Unheard voices

Terror on Muslims

Restless souls

Guns and bullet holes

Wake up America, the enemy has always been here

Chameleon

Kiran Waqar and Hawa Adam

Hi

We are color changing machines

Our survival is camouflage

We have to adapt

I don't mean to brag but if there was an award for best
assimilator, I think I would win

Actually, no, we would win

We are the queens of chameleons, the rulers of all

We have so many different layers we don't even know
who we are

Who we are

Who we are

Who we are

Layer #1: The epidermis, its use: Protection

Protecting us from ignorant predators

Your skin is too dark for the playground

Silent objections

And isolating stares

But it is not a shell

It cannot hide us

It cannot keep us safe

So we develop thick skin so no one can ever see us

So no one can ever know us

Including ourselves

Layer #2: The chromatophore

The layer which contains yellow and red pigments

Yellow for the sun,

A blazing fire that my skin can handle, was born to handle

Red for the blood my eyes have always witnessed

My big eyes

They move independently, but always seem to work together

They are always aware

Looking in all directions

Traditional and contemporary

Looking, searching, examining

Who will I be today? Who will I try to please today?

Whose name will my sticky tongue try to grasp next?

Layer #3: Our melanophore layer,

The carrier of darkness

Melanin

coding for the brown and blacks

We use it when we're around our darker surroundings

Hiding away so no one knows we're here

In our lighter surroundings we use

Layer: #4: the nether layer, which only reflects

white.

We will never be white

Only pretend to be

We hide behind fake mirrors and lies, unsure of who
we really are

Am I African American or the other way around?

Pakistani first? American?

When the tears roll down our face

Droplets form a perfectly-curved rainbow

Red

Orange

Yellow

Green

Blue

Purple

Which one am I?

Which one are we?

Maybe we are a mix

Maybe we are many

A combination of colors never heard before

Maybe we are one

Labels

Labels.

Labels represent a way of differentiating and identifying people.

Little do they know, they are demeaning those they are describing or classifying.

Do they know that labeling the minority is impacting us negatively?

Society seems to be focused on negatively labeling those who might be seen as deviant from cultural norms.

The funny thing is, behaviors are deviant only when society labels them as deviant.

Labeling is adaptive and miraculous, but it also contributes to some of the deepest problems that face our species.

So what makes us any different from you?

Is it the way I dress?

The way I talk?

The way I hush my voice from the crowd?

Or the way I raise my voice aloud?

How are we distinguished?

I remember when I was a little girl my mama taught me that we are all human, but all different beings

So if we are all trying to be different, doesn't that make us the same?

I remember asking my father the same question

He said to me; "this is a baby he doesn't hate anyone because of their religion, creed, gender,

or appearance. He doesn't hate anyone because he doesn't understand the concept. So don't show him it, don't let him hear it, don't teach it to him."

So why is society is so used to labeling the minority?

Is it because we aren't meeting the unbearable standards of society?

Or is it because we aren't keeping up with the latest fashion or Kardashians?

These standards are slowly killing the humanity, and defeating the love for oneself.

Just because we are all different, it doesn't mean we don't experience the same obstacles

Or emotions like anger, fear, happiness, sadness, disgust, surprise, or neutral.

So please, tell me society if we're all the same who gave you the authority to label one another?

Did you know that if we line up 100 people across a room, none of them would share the exact same skin tone?

Yet the continuity of skin tone has not stopped humans from assigning each other to discrete skin color categories like "black" and "white"

Categories that go on to determine the social, political, and economic well-being of others

Who gave you the idea that we will not be impacted by these demeaning terms?

Because if you don't think there are people depressed, harming themselves, angry with themselves, or killing themselves due to these labels, then you better get yourself checked.

Because it's not easy going through the day believing you are the words society has stabbed you with their tongue.

Because these are the words that define ourselves in the worst possible way

But me?

Don't think that these labels will push me down

Because I will fight

I will fight through every word thrown at me

I will fight through every popular misconception

Because contrary to popular belief I will not come to your neighborhood and blow everything up, I will not terrorize innocent souls, or any souls,

But what I will do is remove my label, rip it up, and throw it away

Because I know who I am

Not society.

Balance Beam

Hawa Adam

Gym class 2009

A young girl steps in to face her biggest fear yet

She thinks to herself

Nothing can hold her back from this kind of success

Can tell her she can't do it

Can scare her away

Nothing, but the balance beam

She hops on to it hoping that it would be just as easy
for her as it was for the other kids

She wishes for one single chance to prove to the rest
that she could maintain balance

She crosses her fingers that no one would laugh

Little does she know that with one foot comes the
stumbling of another

That we are not all as nimble as Jack

That this beam was not made for victory on her part

There never seems to be victory on her part only obstacles

But she dodges these obstacles

No, bullets, its Matrix

Puts on costumes to make everyone comfortable

it's White Chicks

Doesn't know how to choose one thing over the other

Twilight, Eclipse

I'm sorry I didn't mean to critique my life as a movie

but now it seems I can't separate fantasy from reality

All my energy is concentrated on what I can't have

And what I do have is something most can't handle,

I can't handle

I'm black,

I'm proud to be black,

Scared to be black,

I'm black.

They tell me I'm beautiful in my skin, but how far does beauty roll off your tongue.

They tell me that diversity is what completes their community

Accepting is different from tolerating.

They tell me I will never again be considered below them but our bodies have sunk before.

You engulf us whole still assuming we'll make it in time for a breath of air.

And it takes no time for you to swivel your head around

and look at me whenever slavery is mentioned.

Is black blood the only blood that is visible?

Look at me.

I'm not only black, I'm Muslim.

I brush those terrorist jokes off my back.

But all the body is connected

In front of the back is the heart.

Though you may not see it, my heart just died a little.

And yes these are the jokes that you and your friends whisper as if I am blind, deaf, mute.

Honey, I would respond If I could.

But I have been taught that silence is sometimes better.

But I can't stay silent when Islam is our new unit in school,

Did you need help pronouncing the words Koran, Haaj, and Al-lah?

By the way its Quran, Hajj, and Allah

My point is when I'm not running away from sirens

warning me

Get away you don't belong because you're black

I'm running away from the voices telling me

You clearly don't belong, you're Muslim

I'm convinced that there are two TV screens in my house

and when one is off, the other automatically goes on.

You see white folks never hesitate to tell black, Muslim people who they are and what they do.

Sometimes I shift my weight to one side of the scale because I appreciate one part of me over the other.

Will I ever appreciate both simultaneously?

It's hard enough being one color,

One person,

One identity,

Imagine being two

And no this is not a cry for help

You had your chance

I'm not some child screaming for stupid attention,

You didn't dare look

This is not just a poem informing you of what you do,

You already know

This is me telling you that my life isn't Hannah Montana, it's not the best of both worlds,

This is me telling you

That my voice is the only thing that matters anymore

And I'm going to use my voice

To tell you that I'm both

Black,

Muslim

In a world where it's hard,

No! Exhausting to find balance on a balance beam

Cognitive Dissidence

Lena Ginawi

You've been lied to.

Some have said we are going to make America great again.

But, how can we be great when

our politicians buy cars with money they haven't earned

to impress people, they have no love for?

Our people unify only when they have something to fear.

They fear the unknown.

Islam is the unknown.

Muslims are the unknown.

Radical. Muslims.

They take the name of Islam and stain it with bloodshed.

Is this all you see when you hear the name of my religion?

How can you hate me this much when we've never even spoken?

Islamophobia is suffocating, the saturation is enough.

I've had enough--

Because Islam to me is a path to peace.

We spend our days in prayer,

Five times a day shoulder to shoulder.

Have you ever read the hadiths where the Prophet Muhammad (SAW) shows love and kindness even to those who treat him ill?

Have you ever even opened the Quran and let the words of the divine wash over you in melodic harmony?

The Prophet Muhammad taught peace even in times of war and conflict.

I can identify

I write words that spell peace

But if it has taken people centuries to hear the Prophet's message of mercy, how long will it take them to hear me?

The Quran teaches how our Lord is Most Merciful

America, it is never too late to repent.

America, you lied to me

You called yourself united and gave me false hope

But it's never too late to remember that we are all human

We should share the commonality of yearning,

get to know each other.

We are all equal.

But some are more equal than others

Aren't they?

I turn on the news

I try to understand, but we fight and we argue

and we aren't doing anything to stop it.

We throw opinions like punches,

spilling out words like blood,

but nobody listens.

I am sickened that America has made this the new normal

I'm tired of fighting

Tired of mourning

tired of wet skin and sore eyes

I'm tired

What do we do?

Do we change our regulations? Admit our sickness?

Do we shrink into a little ball, or straighten up?

Maybe to move forward we need to go back through
the creased pages of time

To where the prophet reveals his wisdom.

Maybe we are in the darkness before the dawn.

We are blind to one another -

Afraid of one another -

We see shadows and demons where there are none.

But I can see Allah in the sunrise!

When will we rise like his great creation and find
ourselves standing together.

Speak

Kiran Waqar

What makes us any different than a mountain lion?

A bumble bee?

A bat? A monster?

Is it our opposable thumbs?

The ability to understand the world around us?

The corny dad jokes?

The motherly affection?

What makes us human? What changes us from beast to person?

It is our voices

Our opinions that invoke change

That are heard from the tops of mountains

From the darkest corners where not even light can escape

We are there. We are brave. We are loud. We are unbashful. We are quiet

Whispering our beliefs

Right

Wrong

Yes

No

We are the change

With every breath

Stance

Opinion we alter the course of humanity

We screw the road map of society

Searching the busy roads for beautiful gems

The quiet streets for hidden messages

The forgotten allies for the forgotten folks

Every day we choose our words

Whether we support bigotry or love

Hate or peace

Joy or anger

We fight against the blanket of silence

Surrounding us

Suffocating us

Killing us

We use the daggers of our tongues to cut away the masks of society

That we should not, must not, cannot speak the crimes against the silenced.

Unless you wish to join their ranks

Do not speak of white privilege, racism, sexism, Islamophobia

You will not

You will not make them uncomfortable

You will not wake their consciousness.

They cannot be subjected to the truth

The reality that we face

So they silence us turning our experiences into myths

Dismissing us based on our sexuality, color, gender or race

A woman should know her place

Don't speak unless spoken to

Stay quiet- don't cause problems

Shhhhhh

Your words could mean your life

But I refuse

I will shout from the rooftops

I will bright light to the hidden shadows

To the stories swept under the rug

The tales hidden in the back of closets

The truths of the crimes against my people and yours

I will stand here, against world poverty

Against rape

Against hatred

I will stand here proud to support

Justice

Love

And equal opportunity

I will not only stand in silence I will speak

I will roar and I will shout

For the minute they take our voices away we become
the beast.

An animal which can be abused, mistreated and killed.

So yell, scream, shout!

Let no one silence you!

Fight until the words can no longer be formed on your lips

Until the eloquent sentences have be reduced to ragged breath

Speak until the world shakes under the might of your words

Speak until those who tried to silence you are scared when you crack your lips

Speak with power

Speak wisely

Speak

Voices

Kiran Waqar, Hawa Adam, Lena Ginawi, Balkisa Abdikadir

I can't talk about black liv…

Shhhhhh

Don't talk about it

There is an elephant in the room

I can't talk about gay righ...

Shhhhh don't talk about it

There is an elephant in the room

I am in my room

Watching video

After video

After video

Black girl talks about black power

White girl talks about feminism

Muslim girl recites the Quran

Hmmmm

I want to hear a white person speak up against racism

I want to see a man stand up against rape

I want to witness a Jew preach against Islamophobia

Does this even happen?

Why isn't this happening?

There is an elephant in the room

These problems are too big for one group to handle

One person

One identity to handle

We need you

And you need us

Slavery was not ended by black people alone

It took an arson of colors

These conflicts transcend me

Me

Me

Me

Us

Our voices need to join together

Loud and in **unison**

We're not black but we support black lives matter.

Let's meet at 6:30 tomorrow.

We should meet with Ebony

Don't forget their support is vital...

Wait. Listen. In order for our voices to join together you must listen.

It means you listen

It does not mean you understand these issues better than me.

It does not mean you can speak for me

It does not mean that a man can speak in place of a woman's body

That a cisgender person can speak for a transgender person

It means, educate yourselves

Take the time to break the barriers

Listen to the language until your heart becomes a fluent speaker

Hear my words,

Feel my pain,

Then tell my story

Because there is a fine line between supporting my problems and saying you experience my problems

There is an elephant in the room

We need to break the silence!

Please

Step outside of your comfort zone

Make the effort to learn about these issues

Saying you know is not enough

Know with your heart

Feel it

It's beating

Feel it

It's ours.

www.ingramcontent.com/pod-product-compliance
Lightning Source LLC
Chambersburg PA
CBHW031616040426
42452CB00006B/553